# THE 10
# Deadliest Snakes

Jennifer Meghan Jenkins

Series Editor
**Jeffrey D. Wilhelm**

Much thought, debate, and research went into choosing and ranking the 10 items in each book in this series. We realize that everyone has his or her own opinion of what is most significant, revolutionary, amazing, deadly, and so on. As you read, you may agree with our choices, or you may be surprised — and that's the way it should be!

an imprint of
**SCHOLASTIC**

www.scholastic.com/librarypublishing

A Rubicon book published in association with Scholastic Inc.

 © 2007 Rubicon Publishing Inc.
www.rubiconpublishing.com

All rights reserved. No part of this publication may be reproduced, stored in a database or retrieval system, distributed, or transmitted in any form or by any means, electronic, mechanical, photocopying, recording, or otherwise, without the prior written permission of Rubicon Publishing Inc.

 is a trademark of The 10 Books

SCHOLASTIC and associated logos and designs are trademarks and/or registered trademarks of Scholastic Inc.

Associate Publishers: Kim Koh, Miriam Bardswich
Project Editor: Amy Land
Editor: Teresa Carleton
Editorial Assistants: Sandeep Punia, Nikki Yeh
Creative Director: Jennifer Drew
Project Manager/Designer: Jeanette MacLean

The publisher gratefully acknowledges the following for permission to reprint copyrighted material in this book.

Every reasonable effort has been made to trace the owners of copyrighted material and to make due acknowledgment. Any errors or omissions drawn to our attention will be gladly rectified in future editions.

"Warning! Be Alert!" An excerpt from "Survivors of Taipan Bite,"
by Ann Wakefield. © Queensland Museum. Used with permission.

"Schoolboy survives lethal snake bite," by Barbara Cole,
*The Daily News*, November 8, 2005. Used with permission.

"Snake Slaughter," courtesy of Mark O'Shea.

Cover: Death Adder–Photo by Ian Waldie/Getty Images

**Library and Archives Canada Cataloguing in Publication**

Includes index.
ISBN 978-1-55448-472-0

1. Readers (Elementary) 2. Readers–Snakes I. Title II. Title: Ten Deadliest Snakes

PE1117.J445 2007a        428.6        C2007-902002-X

1  2  3  4  5  6  7  8  9  10   10   16 15 14 13 12 11 10 09 08 07

Printed in Singapore

# Contents

Introduction: Watch Out! ... 4

## Inland Taipan ... 6
Watch your step — you don't want to provoke this nasty snake.

## Tiger Snake ... 10
Don't call this snake a picky eater. It can eat a wide range of animals from frogs to birds.

## Death Adder ... 14
This killer snake has definitely earned its name. To attract prey, it mimics an innocent worm and then bam! The death adder will strike its surprised victim!

## Coastal Taipan ... 18
What happens when the coastal taipan bites a human being? Try blurred vision, stomach cramps, and severe headaches.

## Eastern Brown Snake ... 22
It doesn't have large fangs and it's not very big — seems harmless, right? Guess again — it has the second most potent venom in the world.

## Black Mamba ... 26
Magical or not, this fast-moving snake is one clever mastermind — don't leave your car doors open!

## Common Krait ... 30
This night-loving snake has the highest fatality rate of any snake on record.

## Saw-Scaled Viper ... 34
Don't underestimate this snake. It may be small, but its ferociousness will amaze you.

## Indian Cobra ... 38
There's more to this charming creature than meets the eye.

## Russell's Viper ... 42
A snake that even scientists are afraid of, this viper will attack you in the time it takes for you to blink an eye.

## We Thought ... 46
## What Do You Think? ... 47
## Index ... 48

# Watch Out!

They slither through tall grass, across sand, and over rocks. Some can climb trees and others can outswim most fish. They hiss, they rattle, they shed their skin, and they don't blink. Since they don't have arms or legs, they can't be much of a threat to us humans — right? Wrong! With their needle-sharp fangs and lightning-quick reflexes, snakes can inject a deadly cocktail into unsuspecting victims.

There are over 2,700 species of snakes in the world, but only about 500 of them are venomous. That might seem like a small number, but these snakes can do some serious damage. Snakes bite over 300,000 people each year. Even with modern medical treatment, every year between 40,000 to 100,000 people still die worldwide from snakebites. What do all of the victims of snakebites have in common? They experience a lot of pain and their lives are put at risk — but if they survive, they are the lucky ones!

A lot of factors contribute to making a snake deadly, including its size, the length of its fangs, its aggressiveness, what it eats, where it lives, and most importantly, the power of its venom. In this book, we present what we think are the 10 deadliest snakes. As you read about these slithery creatures ask yourself:

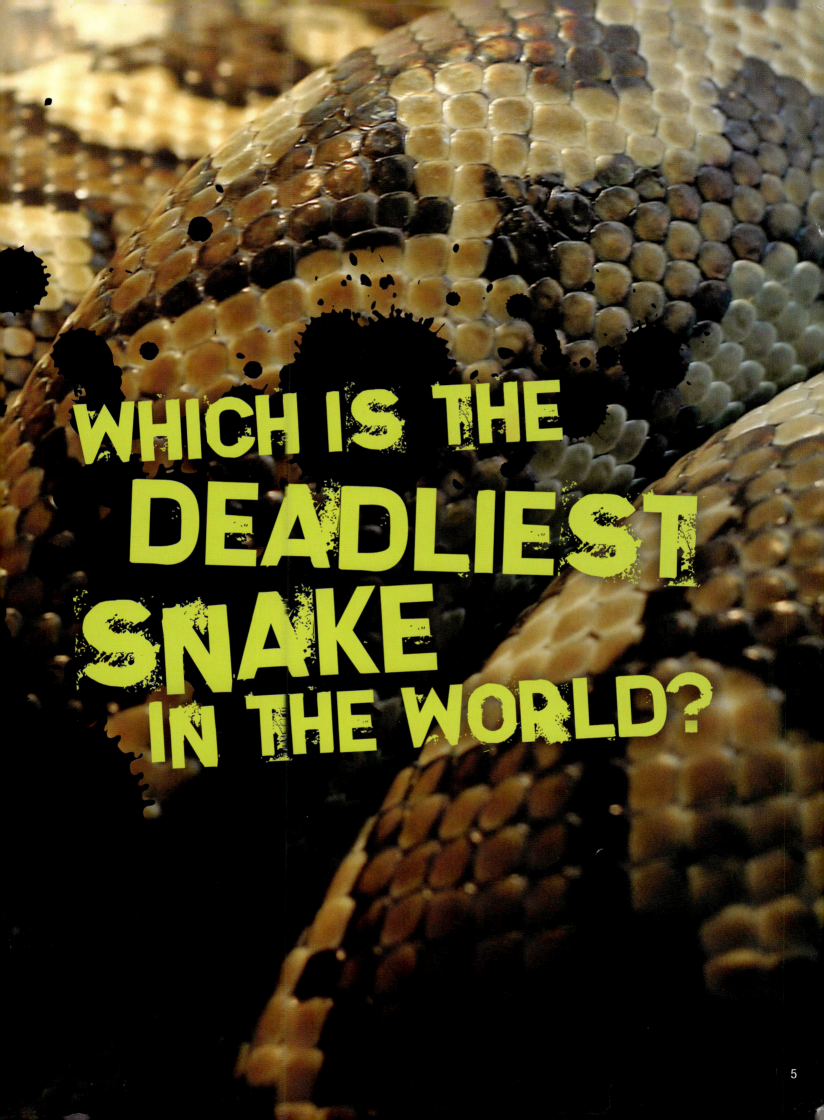

# 10 INLAND TAIPAN

*Watch your step in the outback —
you might meet this deadly creature.*

INLAND TAIPAN–PHOTO COURTESY MARK O'SHEA

# AN

**LENGTH:** Up to 8 feet

**FEAR FACTOR:** This snake has a lightning-fast bite, which can deliver the most powerful venom of any land snake on Earth.

This snake definitely feels the need for speed! The inland taipan (ti-pan) is super-fast, smooth-slithering, and stubborn, making it one of the deadliest snakes in Australia.

Most snakes bite their prey and then release it, waiting patiently for it to die. But when the inland taipan bites, it holds on. Although very few human bites have been documented, its venom is so deadly that one bite is enough to kill 100 people or 250,000 mice. A lot of the time victims don't even realize that the snake is around until they have been bitten.

Turn the page to find out why this sneaky snake is #10 on our list …

# INLAND TAIPAN

## DANGEROUS DWELLINGS

People visiting the Australian outback had better watch their step. The inland taipan is found in isolated parts of Central Australia. It loves hot, dry climates, and prowls the region's dusty plains, ashy downs, and grasslands. It sleeps in deep cracks in the earth and in the burrows of small mammals.

 The snake lives far away from human settlement. Why does this increase the chance of a person dying if he or she is bitten by it?

## IF LOOKS COULD KILL

The inland taipan has a glossy black head and a mustard yellow body that's often covered with faint, dark specks. It comes in several color variations, from dark brown to light straw. The color of its body changes to adapt to the seasons (darker in winter and lighter in summer).

downs: *areas of chalky land*

 Why do you think the inland taipan changes color?

## CHOW TIME

Without any arms or legs, a snake trying to eat something that is alive (and struggling) can be quite, *um*, challenging. That's where the taipan's extremely powerful venom comes in handy. Its favorite victims are the rats that are abundant in Australia. When hunting, the inland taipan dives headfirst into rat burrows, sinking its fangs into its juicy prey. It lets its venom kill the animal before swallowing it whole.

## WHAT DO THEY DO?

This snake gives new meaning to eating someone out of house and home. It spends most of its day resting in rat burrows — after eating the original occupant! On the other hand, humans don't have to worry as much as rats do. The inland taipan is so shy that the only known bites to humans have been to people who keep them as pets or who search for them in the wild.

### Quick Fact
Venom from the inland taipan is more toxic than that of any other land snake in the world. It can kill by paralyzing the respiratory system.

### The Expert Says...
"If you are bitten, don't panic. Sheer terror causes many of the worst effects, and probably kills some people even if the snake is harmless."

— Richard Shine, **herpetologist**

herpetologist: *zoologist specializing in the study of reptiles and amphibians*

*One of the inland taipan's favorite meals is rats.*

**10** 9 8 7 6

# HOW TO ADMINISTER FIRST AID TO A SNAKEBITE VICTIM

Is there a doctor in the house? If not, this report will help you treat someone who has been bitten.

It may sound gross, but some people believe that the way to treat a snake bite is to cut open the victim's wound and suck out the venom. Don't do this! Scientists now agree that this can do more harm than good. Think about it. If you have any cuts in your mouth, you are allowing the venom to enter your bloodstream — you've just made yourself a victim too.

There is one thing that all doctors and scientists agree on when treating snakebite victims: you shouldn't attempt to catch or kill the snake. You are wasting valuable time, and chances are good that you will be bitten yourself.

Your chances of getting up close and personal with an inland taipan are probably slim. But just in case you ever come into contact with a venomous snake, you need to know how to administer first aid to a snakebite victim. Read the yellow list for some instructions we hope you'll never have to use.

1. Keep the victim calm.
2. Have him or her lie down and remain still.
3. Keep the limb that was bitten from moving. Don't apply tight bandages that cut off the circulation.
4. Get the patient to the hospital as soon as possible. A doctor must treat the victim with antivenom.
5. Notify the doctor of any signs or symptoms that you notice in the victim, such as drooping eyelids, slurred speech, sweating, or chills.

## Take Note

The inland taipan has the most toxic venom of any snake, yet it only ranks as #10 on our list. Sure, one bite from this snake can kill a full-grown human. Yet very few people are ever bitten by an inland taipan. This is because this solitary snake makes its home far from human settlement.
• How important is contact with humans when determining the deadliness of a snake?

# 9 TIGER SNAKE

*This snake is very territorial and will live in the same home for years.*

**LENGTH:** 3 to 6.5 feet

**FEAR FACTOR:** This tiger doesn't have claws and massive jaws like the big cat that shares its name. That doesn't mean it can't kill you, though.

Sure, you could say that the tiger snake was given its name because its stripes resemble those of a tiger. But, even though not all tiger snakes have stripes, they do all have the power to strike fear in the hearts of people. The tiger snake's fangs and deadly venom are a lethal combination.

A tiger hunts by carefully stalking its prey, circling as closely as possible, and then suddenly charging from behind. A tiger snake uses the same surprise tactic. If it's in the area, you won't know until it's too late. To make matters worse, this snake doesn't want to hide in the jungle like a scaredy-cat. It wants to live right where you do. So you'd better watch out! Want to know where the tiger snake lives? Turn the page to find out.

**?** Which animal do you think is more threatening to people — the tiger or the tiger snake? Why?

# TIGER SNAKE

## DANGEROUS DWELLINGS
This snake lives in the most highly populated region of Australia. It loves areas with water, so it can be found in the swamps, wetlands, and watercourses in the southeastern part of the continent. Some snakes like solitude. Not this one. If there is a lot of food around, there will also be a lot of tiger snakes.

## IF LOOKS COULD KILL
Yes, some tiger snakes have stripes — but not all of them. This snake can be hard to recognize from color alone. It can be a solid jet-black, gray, olive-brown, or even a yellowish-orange. If the snake has bands, these bands can be gray, brown, or cream. The tiger snake has a short, muscular body with a broad head.

## CHOW TIME
The tiger snake isn't a picky eater. It will eat birds, lizards, small mammals, other snakes, frogs, and occasionally fish. Frogs are its favorite treat. When it is really hot out, it eats mostly at night. Otherwise, it prefers to eat during the day.

## WHAT DO THEY DO?
This snake uses two methods to kill its prey. Like other venomous snakes, it uses its fangs to inject a toxic poison into its victim. But it doesn't stop there! It also uses constriction to kill its food. After the snake has bitten its prey, it constricts the victim by coiling around its body. Then the snake swallows it whole.

constricts: *squeezes; presses together*

### Quick Fact
The tiger snake is a protected species. If you kill or injure one, you could be fined up to $4,000.

**?** Why do you think the Australian government would want to protect a deadly snake from extinction?

*The tiger snake can climb trees to raid birds' nests.*

## The Expert Says...
On the dangers of keeping a tiger snake:

" They often bite their keepers. As juveniles [young snakes] it's not usually too bad; your hand just swells up to the size of a football. But once they hit over 20 inches, they can kill you. The reason they often nail keepers is that they are unpredictable … "

— Scott Eipper, snake keeper

# DANGEROUS JOB!

**A**re you looking for a job that has action, adventure, and the threat of death? Why not try your hand at milking a snake? Snake venom can be worth more than gold. You can sell your treasure to antivenom manufacturers and research labs. For example, it has been used for treating breast cancer, some viruses, heart attack, and Alzheimer's disease. Of course, you do have to handle venomous snakes every day, and you might be bitten. This is why only trained experts can handle this job. How much money can you make from a snake's deadly brew? That depends on many factors, including how hard the snake is to milk, how much venom it produces, and how easy it is to keep in captivity. The list below shows the price of one gram of snake venom for the top 10 deadliest snakes.

## PRICE OF SNAKE VENOM:

| | |
|---|---|
| Inland taipan | $1,450 |
| Tiger snake | $1,500 |
| Death adder | $850 |
| Coastal taipan | $1,400 |
| Brown snake | $4,250 |
| Black mamba | $650 |
| Common krait | $1,600 |
| Saw-scaled viper | $2,000 |
| Indian cobra | $250 |
| Russell's viper | $2,800 |

(prices may vary)

A gram is tiny. It is equal to 0.035 ounce.

### Quick Fact

When threatened, the tiger snake flattens its neck to form a small hood similar to the one cobras display.

### Take Note

Unlike the solitary inland taipan, #10 on our list, the tiger snake lives near people. In a hot country like Australia, humans enjoy spending time near water, and unfortunately, so does this snake, which comes in at #9.
- Why do you think the tiger snake's temperament and its choice of food and habitat make it more dangerous than the inland taipan?

TIGER SNAKE - © ROBERT VALENTIC/NATURE PICTURE LIBRARY; ALL OTHER IMAGES-SHUTTERSTOCK, ISTOCKPHOTO

# 8 DEATH ADDER

*Bites from the death adder, if left untreated, may be fatal.*

**LENGTH:** 18 to 38 inches

**FEAR FACTOR:** With a name like death adder, you know that this snake must be dangerous!

The death adder has a history of striking fear into people's hearts. Most snakes go out looking for prey. The death adder waits for prey to come to it. It is a master of the sneak attack. You won't even know that this snake is in the area — then, wham! Out of the blue you are bitten!

Once you are bitten, you had better run. This snake isn't the type to bite and then flee the scene of the crime. It will bite you again and again until you stop struggling.

Turn the page to find out how this tricky snake attracts its prey.

# DEATH ADDER

### DANGEROUS DWELLINGS
The death adder is common across Australia, eastern Indonesia, and New Guinea. It isn't picky about where it lives. It will make its home in rain forests, woodlands, bushes, and even farmers' fields. It likes to lie under piles of leaves, rocks, thick grasses, or rubble.

**Why does this make the death adder more dangerous to people?**

### IF LOOKS COULD KILL
This short snake has a thick, muscular body that thins out into an extremely narrow tail. It has a broad, triangular head. The death adder can be found in a variety of colors, ranging from gray to red, brown, greenish-gray, and even yellow. Its body is marked with irregular narrow bands. Its narrow tail ends with a sharp spine that can be black, white, or cream.

*The death adder has one of the fastest strikes in the world.*

### CHOW TIME
A hungry death adder will eat reptiles, birds, frogs, and small mammals. It attracts prey by wiggling the tip of its tail, mimicking a worm. Unsuspecting targets willingly approach the snake, expecting a tasty meal. Then all of a sudden the snake strikes, injecting toxic venom into the poor creature. In an instant, the hunter becomes the hunted.

### WHAT DO THEY DO?
This unpredictable snake will strike without warning. It lies camouflaged under leaves or other objects, with its tail wrapped around its body just in front of its head. In this position, it can strike quickly when an animal approaches. When it senses danger, the death adder does not flee. Instead, it lies perfectly still, prepared to strike.

---

**mimicking:** *pretending to be something else*
**camouflaged:** *blended in with the environment*

**What other animals use camouflage?**

### The Expert Says...
"An untreated bite has a high death rate. In New Guinea, where we don't have much antivenin [also spelled antivenom], the death rate remains something like 50-50."

— John Weigel, director of the Australian Reptile Park

# ARE YOU AFRAID OF A LITTLE NEEDLE?

**Prepare yourself! This article takes you deep inside the scary mouth of a snake.**

So, how do snakes manage to eat a meal larger than they are themselves without chewing? Or better yet, how do they even catch dinner with no arms or legs?

Snakes have evolved into skillful hunters, thanks to their toxic venom and their sharp fangs. Unlike humans, who have solid teeth, most venomous snakes have hollow fangs. This allows them to inject venom into a victim, much like a doctor injects medicine into a patient with a hypodermic needle. When a snake strikes, it drives its fangs deep into its prey, forcing venom from its glands down into the ducts of the fang and straight into the victim's bloodstream. The venom acts quickly to kill the prey, protecting the snake from injury because the prey dies before it can struggle.

Some snakes have fangs that are stable and stay in the same place in their mouth permanently, like our teeth. This means that their fangs have to be smaller so that they don't pierce the lower jaw when the snake closes its mouth. Other snakes have hinged fangs that fold up in the snake's mouth, swinging forward only when the snake attacks. These fangs are longer, but are more easily damaged when the snake is attacking.

Snakes have rows of teeth in addition to fangs. They don't use them to chew, though. Snakes' teeth are curved backward into their jaws. This helps them eat their victims whole, allowing them to push a meal down their throat without chewing. This could come in handy on those nights when dinner isn't very tasty!

## Quick Fact

Death adders often lie waiting for several days until a meal passes by.

*Skeleton showing snake teeth*

*A snake with grooved fangs*

## Take Note

The death adder's venom is less toxic than that of the tiger snake or the inland taipan, so why does it rank #8? The death adder uses its camouflage to hide undetected, waiting for food to come to it. People can easily step on a death adder without seeing it, and wind up being the recipient of a nasty bite.
• Compare the hunting methods of the tiger snake and the death adder. Which one do you think is deadlier to humans?

5      4      3      2      1

# 7 COASTAL TAIP[AN]

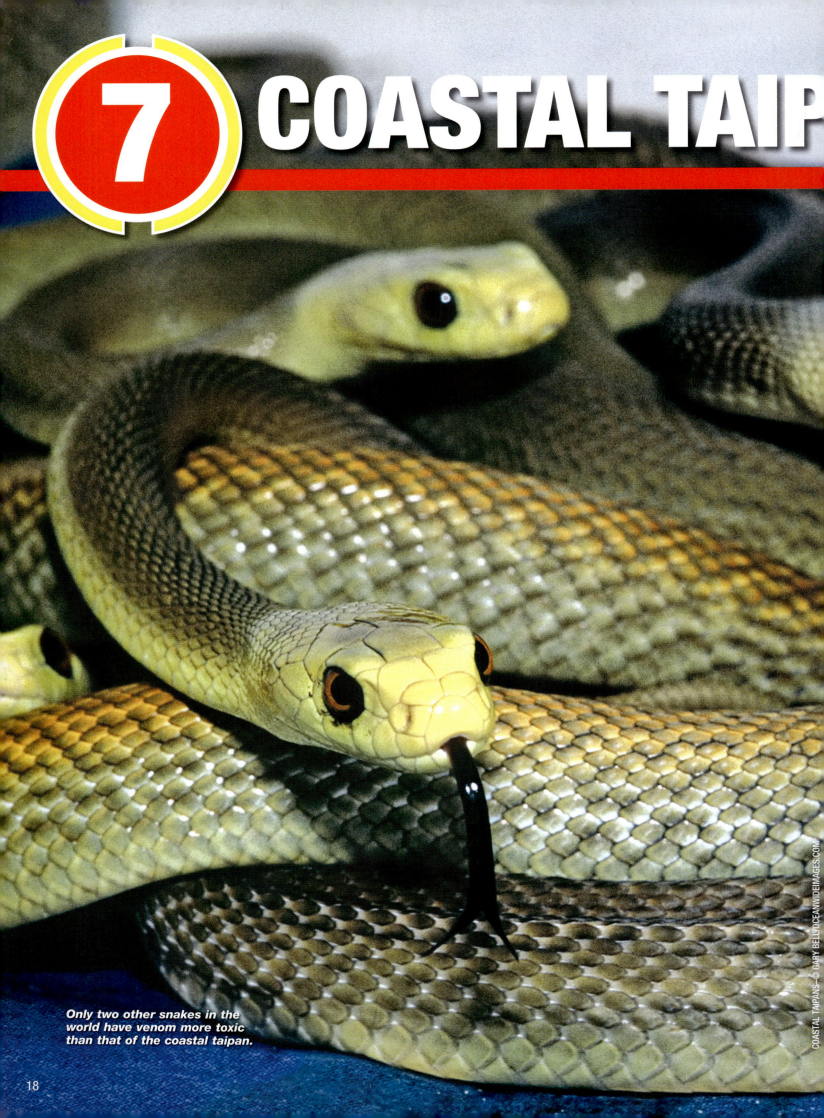

*Only two other snakes in the world have venom more toxic than that of the coastal taipan.*

**LENGTH:** 8 to 12 feet

**FEAR FACTOR:** Do not disturb! Although this snake shares the taipan name with #10 on our list, the coastal taipan is much deadlier. It has a nasty attitude and some huge venom sacs to back it up.

The Australians have a saying: "If you tread on a black snake, it will turn and bite you. Tread on a taipan and it already has." The coastal taipan has a lot in common with its relative the inland taipan, which ranks #10 on this countdown. Both snakes are famous for their lightning-quick reflexes and amazing speed. Both have incredibly toxic venom that can easily kill a person, but nobody would say that the coastal taipan is quiet or shy. This is a nervous, active snake that does not like to be disturbed. To make matters worse, the coastal taipan makes its home near human settlements. Also, it is built to hunt much larger mammals than the inland taipan.

Turn the page to find out more reasons that the coastal taipan is a snake to be feared.

# COASTAL TAIPAN

## DANGEROUS DWELLINGS

The coastal taipan likes the hot, wet climate of southern New Guinea, northern Queensland, and the Northern Territory in Australia. It lives in open forests with few trees, dry closed forests with many trees, coastal heaths, and grassy beach dunes. It also loves to prowl through cultivated corn, sugar cane, and cattle fields where people work. It likes to sleep in leaf piles and rubble heaps.

 **How is this snake's habitat different from the other snakes so far?**

## IF LOOKS COULD KILL

This large snake comes in a variety of colors, ranging from yellow to light olive, reddish brown, dark brown, and black. It is noticeably paler on its sides and stomach. With its reddish eyes shining in the sunlight, it looks like a creature from a horror movie.

**heaths:** *areas with low shrubs*

 **Which of the coastal taipan's physical characteristics make it better at hunting larger mammals than the inland taipan?**

## CHOW TIME

Like the inland taipan, the coastal taipan feasts entirely on mammals. It prefers more variety in its diet than its relative does. Its favorite snack is the bandicoot, but it will eat other small marsupials.

## WHAT DO THEY DO?

The coastal taipan has the longest fangs of any Australian snake. It also has enormous venom sacs. It can inject more venom with each bite than the inland taipan. It delivers repeated quick bites and then retreats to a safe distance to wait for its victim to die. The coastal taipan's venom paralyzes the victim's central nervous system, including the lungs. Death occurs quickly.

**marsupials:** *mammals whose young develop in the mother's pouch*

Bandicoot

One bite from this snake can kill up to 12,000 guinea pigs.

**Quick Fact**
The coastal taipan moves fast. It keeps its head high above the leafy floor and uses its sight as much as its smell.

# WARNING! BE ALERT!

An excerpt from a ==first-person account== of a taipan bite
By Ann Wakefield, Cooktown, Australia

Something touched me. I saw nothing till then. Possibly, I just walked too close to the snake. I hadn't *taunted* it. Nothing. When I saw the snake, I knew it was a taipan — the glitter, the color. It was shiny, dark, blackish-tan, a whopping big one, around 8 feet. I realized I'd been bitten when I looked at the mid-calf area of my left leg. There were two tiny little marks close together.

About 10 minutes later, the symptoms started: blurred vision, like looking through *Perspex* with water running on it, and an unbelievable headache. It took 20 minutes to reach the hospital. By then, I had awful stomach cramps and could hardly breathe. There was no pain at the bite for about four hours. When it began, it was awful, very intense. It lasted for six weeks.

Two and a half hours post-bite, semi-conscious, I was in the Intensive Care Unit at Cairns Base Hospital. My kidneys didn't work for three days. After six days, I was discharged, still fragile, from the hospital.

The aftereffects of this bite have been fairly bad. My left leg below the bite is numb, not everywhere, but in a sort of jagged line, perhaps along a nerve. I get severe headaches I didn't have before. I'm also moody, and I wasn't before.

If I could give advice to anyone from this experience, I'd say: Be alert. I never saw the snake till after the bite. The earth was almost bare on that creek crossing. That's the funny thing about this. Taipans can travel very, very fast.

---

taunted: *teased; harassed*
Perspex: *type of hard clear plastic*

## Quick Fact

The coastal taipan has better eyesight than most snakes. It uses its vision and sense of smell to find prey.

## The Expert Says...

"Death is always in the cards when you are bitten by a snake. … You wouldn't walk up to Muhammad Ali and tease him, and likewise you shouldn't mess around with any Australian snakes."

— Bruno Stolze, herpetologist and snake-handler, Bredl's Wonder World of Wildlife

## Take Note

You may be wondering why the coastal taipan ranks #7, higher than the other Australian snakes mentioned so far. There are many reasons. The coastal taipan has evolved to hunt larger mammals. It has huge venom sacs and a tendency to bite more than once. This means that its venom, designed to destroy mammalian tissue, is injected in large quantities. These things make the coastal taipan very deadly to humans.

• What other factors can you find that make this snake deadlier than the death adder?

5    4    3    2    1

# 6 EASTERN BRO

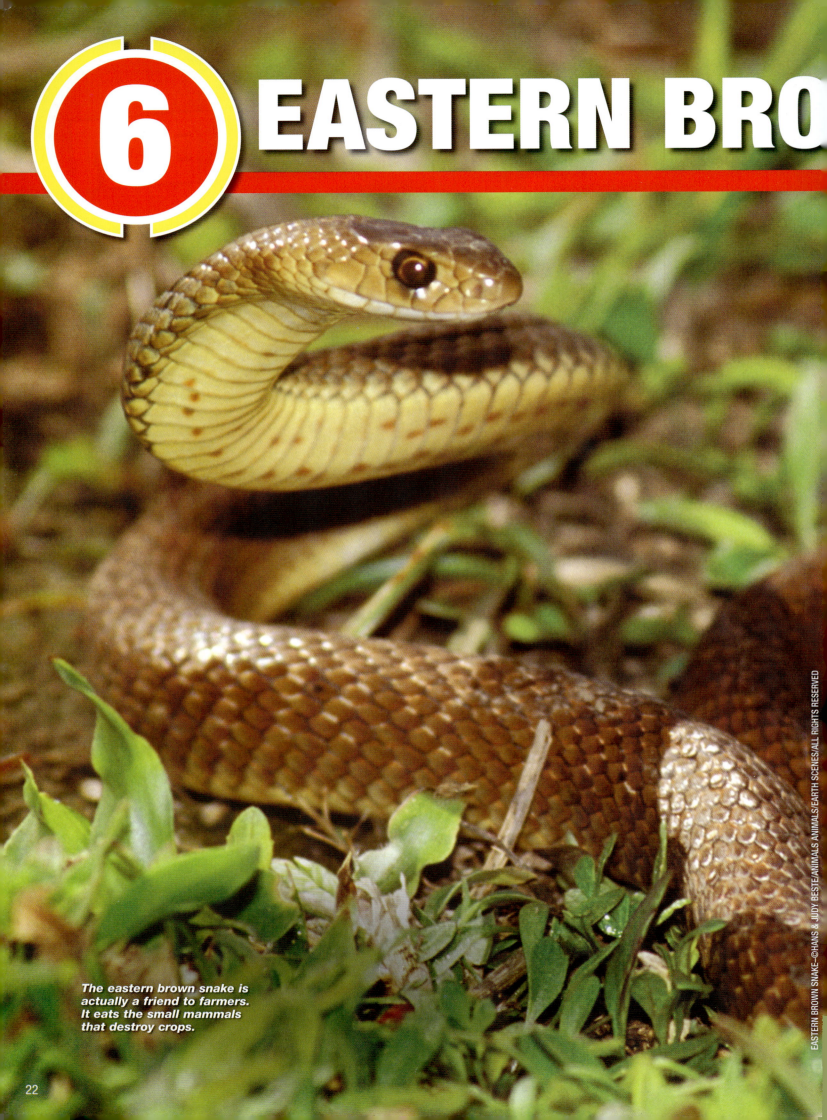

*The eastern brown snake is actually a friend to farmers. It eats the small mammals that destroy crops.*

# WN SNAKE

**LENGTH:** 4 to 7 feet

**FEAR FACTOR:** In Australia, simply walking around in your own backyard can be dangerous. With this snake on the prowl, you always have to watch your step.

This skinny snake may look harmless, but it strikes terror in the hearts of Australians. The eastern brown snake doesn't want to wander around the scorching hot, isolated areas of Australia like the inland taipan. It prefers to be around people, so it lives in the more populated areas of eastern Australia. Are you afraid of snakes and dread seeing one cross your path? Don't worry. You won't see or hear this snake until it is too late.

The eastern brown snake isn't the largest venomous snake in the world. It also doesn't have the largest fangs. What it does have is attitude. This snake is high-strung, easily agitated, and aggressive. It may like to live around humans, but that doesn't mean that it's friendly.

Turn the page to find out why this snake is considered one of the deadliest snakes in Australia.

How do you think scientists decide if a snake is calm and shy or if it is aggressive? Think about some of the ways that you can tell how your friends and family members are feeling. See if these apply to snakes.

# EASTERN BROWN SNAKE

## DANGEROUS DWELLINGS

The eastern brown snake likes to live just where its name implies. It inhabits most of eastern Australia, from the desert to the coast. It can also be found in Papua New Guinea. It prefers open grasslands, pastures, and woodlands, and likes to make its home in piles of rocks, rubble, leaves, and mulch.

## IF LOOKS COULD KILL

If you thought the eastern brown snake was brown, you are partially right. But how many different shades of brown can you name? This snake comes in a variety of colors — anything from tan to dark brown, orange, and black. Its stomach is cream with pink or orange blotches, and it may also have faint black bands.

## CHOW TIME

This snake loves to eat. It will munch on birds, lizards, frogs, and small mammals — anything that resembles food. It has even been known to eat plastic. Many snakes bite their prey and then release it, waiting for it to die. Not the eastern brown snake. It holds on to its victim, until the tasty morsel can't escape.

> ? What are the advantages and disadvantages of this snake's hunting method?

## WHAT DO THEY DO?

Like a lot of snakes, the eastern brown spends its days hunting or basking in the sun. Unfortunately, it likes to be near people. This is the most common type of snake that people in Australia see in their houses and gardens. It usually avoids conflict, but it gets easily upset and is very aggressive when it does. It lifts the front of its body off the ground in an "S" pattern and hisses, preparing to strike.

**Quick Fact**
The eastern brown snake has the second most potent venom of any snake in the world.

> ? Knowing this, why do you think that this snake isn't ranked second on this list of deadly snakes?

*The brown snake is lucky because eastern Australia has had an explosion in the mouse population in recent years.*

**Quick Fact**
Due to its small fangs, a bite from this snake is almost always painless. Often the victim doesn't even see the snake. But this only makes the snake more dangerous.

# A LITTLE SPIT CAN'T HURT YOU, CAN IT?

Human spit may be gross, but a couple drops of it won't kill you. This article reveals the toxic truth about snake venom.

**A**h, the joys of snake venom! Particularly very toxic venom like the eastern brown snake's. Really, venom is nothing more than saliva produced in large glands. Your body produces saliva, but you wouldn't kill anyone by spitting. So what makes snake venom so deadly?

Well, it may be spit, but it is a highly modified toxic form of spit. The clear or yellowish liquid that snakes inject when they bite may be made up of hundreds of proteins and enzymes. Each species of snake has a different mixture geared toward its specific prey or predators. This is why the bites of different snakes have different effects. It also explains why we need different antivenom for each venomous snake, instead of one cure-all drug.

There are two main types of venom — neurotoxins and hemotoxins. Neurotoxins attack the central nervous system, causing paralysis and destroying the respiratory system and the heart. Cobras, mambas, and kraits are examples of snakes that contain mainly neurotoxins. Hemotoxins attack the circulatory system and muscles, causing massive bleeding and destroying muscles. This sometimes leads to amputation of the limbs affected. This type of venom is often found in members of the viper family, which are snakes that have long hinged fangs that penetrate deeply. A lot of snakes, however, use a mixture of both types of venom to kill their prey.

enzymes: *type of chemical produced by the body's cells*

*Eyelash Viper*

## The Expert Says…

" They don't really want to waste their venom on us, but by the same token, if they are provoked they will defend themselves. "

— Rudy Della-Flora, Australian snake catcher

## Take Note

Think back to what you read about the coastal taipan. It sounded like a mean snake, right? Well, the coastal taipan is downright nice compared to the eastern brown snake! The eastern brown snake is easily upset and will defend itself aggressively. It slithers into the #6 spot.

• Why do you think its personality, combined with its physical features, makes the eastern brown snake the deadliest Australian snake on our countdown? Remember, just like people, different snakes have different personalities that affect how they react in scary situations.

5   4   3   2   1

# 5 BLACK MAM

*Watch out! Its venom can kill.*

**LENGTH:** 7 to 13 feet

**FEAR FACTOR:** These snakes have earned themselves a nasty reputation for being vicious killers!

If you talk to many people in Africa, you will soon realize that the black mamba is no ordinary snake. It is described as incredibly fast and super-intelligent, and many legends describe its magical abilities. According to one legend, the black mamba will bite its own tail so that its body forms a circle, which allows it to roll down hills at top speed. Some people say that when the black mamba moves, it creates a whirlwind that destroys everything in its path.

Scariest of all, many people believe that the black mamba plots attacks on people. It is said that the black mamba will lie by the side of the road, waiting for cars. When one passes, it hitches a ride, slithering inside an open window. Once inside, it wraps itself around the steering wheel and savagely attacks the driver.

Many stories are told about the power of the black mamba. The legends aren't true, but many of the stories told about the black mamba are — and what it can do is almost as amazing as the legends.

# BLACK MAMBA

## DANGEROUS DWELLINGS

The black mamba can be found all across the African continent, from Senegal in northern Africa to South Africa. It lives in savannas, semi-arid bush country, open woodlands, and rocky outcrops. It usually likes to make its home in the hollows of trees, old termite mounds, rock crevices, or abandoned mammal burrows.

## IF LOOKS COULD KILL

Most people expect the black mamba to be black, but they're wrong. This snake is actually dark olive, brown, or gray. It is the second longest venomous snake in the world. Only the king cobra is longer. Like the cobra, the black mamba spreads its flat hood to make its head seem larger when it is angry. It does this to scare its opponents.

**outcrops:** *areas of rocks that stick up through the soil*

## CHOW TIME

The black mamba isn't a picky eater. It will feast on rats, mice, squirrels, voles, bushbabies, and other small mammals. It also has very long fangs, which are perfect for biting through birds' feathers.

> **?** Using the other things that the black mamba likes to eat as your clue, what do you think voles and bushbabies are?

## WHAT DO THEY DO?

The black mamba spends lots of time in the sun. It likes to come out in the morning and then hunt for prey. The black mamba tends to be shy and will usually flee at the first sign of humans. However, if it feels threatened, this snake becomes aggressive. It will raise itself more than three feet off the ground, spread its hood, and open its mouth widely, showing its enormous fangs. When attacking, it delivers several quick bites and then lets go of its prey, waiting patiently for it to die.

> **?** Name other creatures you know that become aggressive when threatened.

*The black mamba gets its name from the black lining of its mouth.*

### Quick Fact
The black mamba isn't all bad. Scientists are studying its venom for use as a painkiller.

### The Expert Says ...
"If this creature [black mamba] were to land a bite on me, I would have anywhere from half an hour to four hours to start receiving antivenom. If you don't get the antivenom, you're going to die."

— Jeff Corwin, wildlife biologist, author, lecturer, and Emmy-winning television host

# SCHOOLBOY SURVIVES LETHAL SNAKE BITE

An article from *The Daily News*, November 8, 2005
By Barbara Cole

A 15-year-old Durban [South Africa] schoolboy has survived an encounter with a deadly 10-foot black mamba. But Sibusiso Mseswa would have died if his school had not reacted quickly and immediately called in an ambulance, whose crew then brought in a helicopter to fly him to a hospital.

"You've only got 20 minutes before you stop breathing," said paramedic Asogan Edward, who was onboard the Red Cross Air Mercy helicopter, which is contracted to the provincial health authority and flew the boy to Addington Hospital.

The drama unfolded at Blackburn Primary School in Mount Edgecombe, when Sibusiso was playing soccer.

Although the grass was quite short, Sibusiso did not see the snake and stood on it. He was bitten on the sole of the foot.

The school immediately called an ambulance … and it got to the school within seven minutes, said Edward.

Then, while paramedics applied a tourniquet to prevent the blood circulating around his body, they called in the helicopter, which took 10 minutes to get there from its base at Durban International Airport.

By then, a fellow pupil had killed the snake with a stone. Although Sibusiso had some difficulty breathing as a result of the attack, he was still conscious.

The patient was given antivenom at Addington and is now in the hospital surgical intensive care unit in stable condition.

*The black mamba is the fastest-moving land snake in the world, reaching speeds of up to 14 mph.*

## Take Note

The black mamba is #5 on our list. It is faster, can strike from farther away, and has longer fangs than the eastern brown snake. Before scientists invented antivenom in the 1960s, the black mamba killed 100% of its victims. That is a frightening record!

- The myths that abound about the black mamba certainly show that people are scared of this snake. Do you think people's fears are justified? Explain.

# ④ COMMON KRA[IT]

*The venom of the common krait is 15 times more deadly than the venom of the cobra.*

**LENGTH:** Up to 6 feet

**FEAR FACTOR:** The common krait has the highest fatality rate of any snake on record.

**T**alk about multiple personalities! The common krait acts like two different snakes, depending on when you cross its path. If you're lucky enough to meet it during the day, you'll find that it's quite shy. If it senses danger, it will curl up in a ball with its head concealed and the tip of its tail exposed. When touched, it will flinch, hiss, and make jerky movements. You could poke and prod the snake — and likely come away without a scratch.

Stumble upon this snake at night, though, and you're in for a shock. Suddenly this cowardly snake becomes an aggressive, territorial serpent. Although the common krait would prefer to flee the scene hissing madly, you will get hurt if you corner it.

# COMMON KRAIT

### DANGEROUS DWELLINGS

The common krait can be found throughout India, Pakistan, and Sri Lanka. It lives in open grasslands, scrub jungles, and semi-desert areas. It hides in holes in the ground, but also likes piles of wood, bricks, and debris. Unfortunately for humans, it also likes to seek shelter in sleeping bags, tents, houses, and boots.

### IF LOOKS COULD KILL

The common krait's body color varies from a dark steely blue-black to a pale bluish gray when it is about to slough. Some kraits have about 40 thick white cross bands circling their body, but you would be foolish to try to get close enough to count them!

slough: *shed its skin*

**Quick Fact**

The common krait is often mistaken for the harmless wolf snake.

**?** How could this be helpful for the krait when it is hunting?

### CHOW TIME

Small mammals, such as rats, mice, lizards, frogs, and toads, are on the menu for this snake. The female will stay with the eggs she has laid until they are hatched, but then the babies have to fend for themselves. This cannibalistic snake is not very maternal. It doesn't think twice about eating its young.

### WHAT DO THEY DO?

The common krait is nocturnal, which means that it is mainly active at night. During the day, when it's hot, it relaxes to conserve energy. Once it is dark, this snake goes into hunting mode, prowling the tall grass for a tasty bite. The krait has fairly short fangs compared with other venomous snakes. Don't worry, though. It has found a way to overcome this problem. Instead of landing one quick bite on its victim, the common krait injects its venom by chewing on its prey. And it is a very successful killer!

maternal: *motherly*

**Quick Fact**

The bite of the common krait causes no symptoms at first, and there is little or no pain around the wound. The first symptoms are abdominal cramps, followed by an inability to move. Death occurs six to eight hours later if left untreated.

## The Expert Says...

Captain Suresh Sharma, retired Indian Army officer, popularly known as the "Snakeman," on how to avoid a snakebite:

"Avoid making a rockery in the garden as it attracts the common krait. … At night, always switch on the light before entering a room. Do not put your hands in dark corners because those are snakes' favorite places for shelter."

rockery: *rock garden*

COMMON KRAIT–PHOTO COURTESY MARK O'SHEA. ALL OTHER IMAGES–SHUTTERSTOCK, ISTOCKPHOTO

# BILL HAAST
## WALKING PINCUSHION

**Quick Fact:** The common krait has the highest fatality rate of any snake on record. In one study of 32 victims treated in a hospital, only two people survived.

Most people run when they see a snake — not Bill Haast. Read this profile of a man who has devoted his life to working with all types of deadly snakes, including common kraits.

Now 95 years old, Bill Haast has been described as a walking pincushion, a fact that he is proud of. The founder of the Miami Serpentarium and the Miami Serpentarium Laboratory, Haast has spent more than 50 years handling over three million venomous snakes. In a typical day, Haast will milk as many as 100 snakes, extracting their deadly venom. He then sells the venom to scientists and research labs that work to create antivenom and other lifesaving medicines. He knows that venom can cure illness. In fact, he injects himself with small doses of venom from deadly snakes like cobras, mambas, and kraits. Over time, his blood has developed antibodies that make him almost immune to snake venom. Haast is one of the only people to survive a krait bite. Incredibly, transfusions of his blood have saved at least 21 people.

Of course, being bitten over 150 times by the world's deadliest snakes does have some nasty side effects. A bite from a Siamese cobra left him unable to breathe and landed him in an iron lung for two days. He almost died when a bite from a saw-scaled viper prevented his blood from clotting. Antivenom had to be smuggled in from Iran to save his life that time. His hands have been most injured by the attacks. They are twisted and partially paralyzed due to years of nerve damage from snakebites. In fact, Haast's wife once had to use garden clippers to cut off the tip of one of his fingers after a bite from an eastern diamondback rattlesnake dissolved the tissue, leaving a blackened bone sticking out.

**antibodies:** *chemicals produced by the body that fight disease*
**iron lung:** *airtight metal case fitted over a patient's body, used for lengthy artificial respiration*

### Take Note

The black mamba has earned itself a nasty reputation. It can, and does, kill people. But the common krait earns the #4 spot because it is better at killing. It is very scary that victims of a krait bite do not experience any immediate symptoms or pain around the wound.
• Combined with the other information you have learned in this section, why is the common krait deadlier than the black mamba?

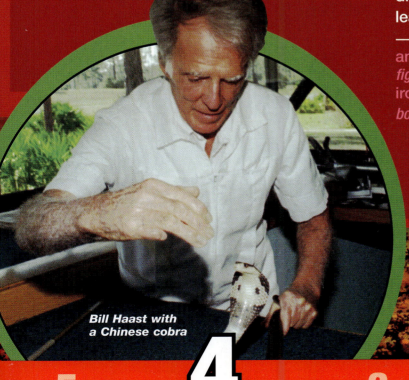
Bill Haast with a Chinese cobra

# ③ SAW-SCALED

*The saw-scaled viper specializes in short, jabbing, rapid bites.*

# VIPER

**LENGTH:** 1.2 to 2.5 feet

**FEAR FACTOR:** You've probably heard that old saying, "It isn't the size of the dog in the fight that matters, but the size of the fight in the dog." That certainly holds true for this small but deadly snake.

It seems as though no one has told the saw-scaled viper that it is small. This snake is as aggressive as they come — and it will let you know when it is angry. All snakes can hiss, and a few can rattle, but this snake has a special trick to warn other creatures not to get too close. Its body is covered with rows of scales that stick out slightly like the teeth on a saw. When it feels threatened, it curls its body into a series of U-shaped curves within one another and rubs its scales together. This makes a surprisingly loud rasping noise that is combined with a loud hiss, telling everyone that it is unhappy.

Sure, it will warn you to back off when it wants to be left alone, but what about when it's on the prowl for its next meal? This snake has a special hunting style that makes it especially dangerous to humans. It won't give you any warning when it is hunting. You won't know what bit you until it's too late. Can you guess what method it uses to catch its dinner? Turn the page to find the answer and more interesting facts about this deadly snake.

rasping: *harsh or scraping sound*

# SAW-SCALED VIPER

## DANGEROUS DWELLINGS

The saw-scaled viper has a large hunting ground, and can be found in highly populated areas of northern Africa, the Middle East, India, and Sri Lanka. It lives in very dry regions and seems to be able to handle the high temperatures of the desert better than most snakes. It is well adapted to life on the sand.

## IF LOOKS COULD KILL

This stocky snake can be brown, red, gray, or sandy-colored, with a darker zigzag pattern across its back and a distinctive cross mark on its head. This coloring acts as a perfect camouflage, allowing it to blend into its desert-like surroundings. Its narrow neck makes its wide head seem even bigger, while its tail is short and stubby.

### Quick Fact

This snake actually stalks its prey! According to reports, this sneaky snake is known to follow its prey for long distances.

## CHOW TIME

The saw-scaled viper will eat mice, lizards, frogs, scorpions, and occasionally other snakes. It hunts by burying itself in the sand, with only its head visible. In this position, it can wait for a tasty morsel to wander by, and then lunge forward, sinking its venomous fangs into its unsuspecting victim. Since it is so well camouflaged in this position, people often get bitten when they step on the snake by accident.

## WHAT DO THEY DO?

This snake is very aggressive and will strike powerfully. When threatened, it coils up like a horseshoe and rubs the sides of its body together in opposite directions to create a sharp sizzling sound. When striking, it may lose its balance and fall in the direction of its victim.

**?** Think of other sounds that snakes, insects, or other animals make to let you know they are in the area.

*Check out this snake's scales. The saw-scaled viper rubs these scales together when it's frightened.*

### Quick Fact

The venom of the saw-scaled viper is both neurotoxic and hemotoxic. Its bite causes breathing problems as well as prevents blood from clotting. Many victims bleed to death before they stop breathing!

## The Expert Says...

"There was one time when I was struck by the most dangerous snake in the world, the saw-scaled viper. This was in 1989. The bite didn't seem serious at first. But the wound wouldn't stop bleeding; my blood just wouldn't clot. It was exciting for a while there."

— Bill Haast, Director, Miami Serpentarium Laboratories

10    9    8    7    6

# SNAKE SNIPPETS

CHECK OUT THESE FACTS FOR A FEW THINGS WE BET YOU DIDN'T KNOW ABOUT THE SAW-SCALED VIPER.

The saw-scaled viper has an average lifespan in captivity of 11 years.

The saw-scaled viper is responsible for more deaths each year than any other snake in the world. In Sri Lanka, it is estimated they are responsible for up to 1,000 deaths every year.

On May 2, 2000, a pet owner in Toronto, Canada, was caught with a pet saw-scaled viper! But don't think he got away with it. Pet owners living in Toronto are fined $225 if they have an illegal exotic pet.

The saw-scaled viper's venom contains powerful anticlotting proteins. Scientists in the United States have used this venom as a model for a "super aspirin" drug that aims to reduce the risk of heart attacks in people.

Watch out! The saw-scaled viper can fling itself almost a foot into the air to deliver a bite. This has led to the myth that the snake can jump.

Heads up! When it rains, saw-scaled vipers climb into trees. Sometimes they can be found up to six feet above the ground.

## Take Note

What makes the saw-scaled viper deadlier than the common krait? Well, it has a lot to do with how the two snakes choose to hunt. The saw-scaled viper lives in a highly populated area, is very well camouflaged, and hunts by hiding in the sand. People can be bitten when they accidentally step on the snake. The common krait hunts mainly at night, when most people are asleep.
- Do you think that the ranking of these two snakes would be reversed if people were nocturnal and moved around more at night?

5    4    **3**    2    1

# 2 INDIAN COBRA

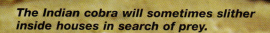

*The Indian cobra will sometimes slither inside houses in search of prey.*

**LENGTH: Up to 6 feet**

**FEAR FACTOR:** This snake is probably the most famous venomous snake in the world. How do you think it got such a deadly reputation? By killing people, of course!

**?** Why do you think snake charmers are willing to handle such a deadly snake? Would you want their job?

**Y**ou've probably seen the Indian cobra on television or in movies, swaying to the music of a snake charmer. You may have thought to yourself that the snake looked peaceful and harmless. Think again. There is nothing safe about this famous snake.

The Indian cobra will let you know if you make it angry. When threatened, it stands its ground, raises up to its full height, spreads its large hood, and stares its soon-to-be victim right in the eye. If you think you can move fast enough to escape this deadly snake, keep dreaming.

Read on for more reasons that the famous Indian cobra weighs in at #2 on our list of deadliest snakes.

# INDIAN COBRA

## DANGEROUS DWELLINGS

As its name suggests, the Indian cobra is found in India. It can also be found in highly populated areas throughout southeast and central Asia, in places like Pakistan, Sri Lanka, and Nepal. This snake lives in rain forests, rice fields, and around human settlements. It often makes its home in the dens of small mammals it has eaten.

## IF LOOKS COULD KILL

Like most snakes, the Indian cobra comes in a variety of colors, from black to dark brown to creamy white. Don't worry about all of the different colors, though. If you cross paths with an Indian cobra, you'll know it. When angered, the Indian cobra flattens the rib bones near its head, spreads out its loose folds of skin, and creates its famous hood.

### Quick Fact
The Indian cobras used by snake charmers often have their fangs or their venom sacs removed, making them harmless to people. However, they often die from diseases and infections due to this.

**?** Do you think it is fair of people to harm the snake for entertainment purposes?

## CHOW TIME

The Indian cobra enjoys munching on a tasty lizard, frog, or juicy rat. When hunting, this snake bites quickly and then waits patiently for its venom to paralyze or kill its prey. This way, it doesn't risk being bitten or scratched. Once the prey can't move, the snake just opens wide and swallows.

## WHAT DO THEY DO?

The Indian cobra can use its large fangs to inject venom. It attacks or defends itself by forcing venom to spray from its fangs. It can hit you from six feet away. If it gets in your eyes, you will experience incredible pain, and you could even go blind.

**?** What advantage do you think the ability to spit its venom gives to this snake?

*The Indian cobra is nicknamed the spectacled cobra because the scales on its hood form two circular patterns, creating what looks like a pair of glasses.*

### The Expert Says...

" [A] snakebite is a traumatic experience that many people in the villages think about more than other diseases. "

— Romulus Whitaker, India's leading herpetologist

### Quick Fact
The Indian cobra is hunted and killed for its skin, which is used to make handbags and other items.

# ARE YOU DYING TO BE FAMOUS?

SOME PEOPLE WILL DO ANYTHING FOR A LITTLE FAME. TAKE A LOOK AT THESE REPORTS OF SOME OF THE CRAZY STUNTS PEOPLE HAVE PERFORMED USING DEADLY SNAKES.

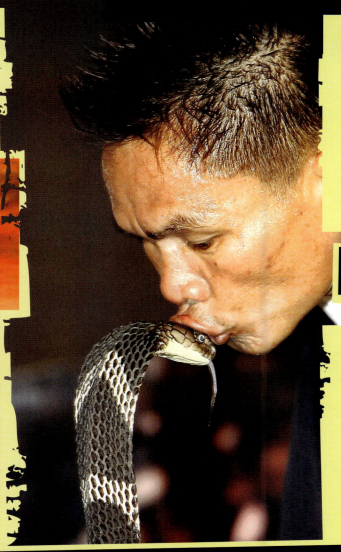

## PUCKER UP

Shahimi Abdul Hamid of Malaysia is famous for kissing a deadly snake — several times! In 2006, this daring man kissed a 15-foot cobra on the head 51 times in just over three minutes. With only his hands as protection, the snake farm supervisor charmed the deadly snake (its venom can kill an elephant in four hours). Who knew kissing could be so dangerous?

## LONGEST TIME SPENT LIVING WITH SNAKES

Boonreung Buachan, a snake fanatic in Thailand, set a record in 1998 by living in a glass box filled with venomous snakes for seven days. The box, placed in a mall in Bangkok, was filled with two king cobras (largest of the cobra family), 100 smaller cobras, 30 centipedes, and 20 scorpions. Buachan only had goggles for protection from venom. While he survived this deadly encounter, Buachan died in 2004 after being bitten by a cobra he was handling. Maybe being famous isn't all it's cracked up to be!

## MOST COBRAS KISSED

A medical team waited on the sidelines as snake charmer Khum Chaibuddee kissed 19 highly poisonous cobras. This attempt to break a world record took place in October 2006 in Thailand. After reminding the audience not to try this at home, Chaibuddee locked lips with each of the 19 cobras as they were released onto the stage.

### Take Note

Like the saw-scaled viper, the Indian cobra lives in heavily populated areas. It is highly venomous, but unlike the saw-scaled viper, it doesn't hide from people. The cobras enter villages in search of a meal, where they come into contact with people.

- Human actions can affect the deadliness of a snake. What other things do people do that can alter the number of victims bitten by a snake?

# 1 RUSSELL'S

**The Russell's viper kills more people each year than any other snake.**

# VIPER

**LENGTH:** Up to 5 feet

**FEAR FACTOR:** Tread on this snake by accident, and you are in for a world of pain. The Russell's viper won't let you walk away without a bite.

What does it take to be ranked #1 on a list of the world's deadliest snakes? Do you need to be the biggest snake or have the most toxic venom? Maybe you need to have the largest fangs or the quickest strike? Well, all of those things are important, but you need more than that to top the list.

The Russell's viper is a large, muscular snake with huge fangs and deadly venom. It bites at breakneck speed. What makes it stand out as the deadliest snake in the world? The sheer number of people it has killed! This snake is a killing machine. It is easily agitated and has a nasty attitude. Even scientists are afraid of this snake. Most snakes give up once they are caught, but not the Russell's viper. It never stops struggling and its quick reflexes and powerful fangs can deliver a deadly bite in the time it takes you to blink.

# RUSSELL'S VIPER

### DANGEROUS DWELLINGS

This snake is common throughout Southern Asia, from Pakistan through to China and Indonesia. It can be found in a variety of habitats, from dense rain forests to farmlands. The Russell's viper loves to hunt in the rice fields that have replaced the forests it used to live in.

> **?** How do you think human settlement has changed the living environment for the Russell's viper and other snakes?

### IF LOOKS COULD KILL

This large snake has a wide, triangular head and wide nostrils. It has a light brown body with three rows of dark brown or black splotches that are bordered with white or yellow. Its stomach is white and may have splotches.

### CHOW TIME

This snake is a meat-eater. It eats mostly rats and other small mammals, but has been known to feast on chicken. It prowls villages and farms looking for an easy meal. This makes it enemy #1 with chicken farmers.

**Quick Fact**
One bite from a Russell's viper is toxic enough to kill 150 people.

*The snake's Chinese name translates to "chain snake." This is because the pattern on its body looks like a chain.*

### WHAT DO THEY DO?

A bite from this snake is extremely painful and deadly. When angered, the Russell's viper hisses loudly and strikes quickly, often holding on to its victim to ensure that all of its venom is injected. Its venom prevents blood from clotting, so the wound oozes blood for hours. Victims experience pain, swelling, vomiting, and dizziness as they bleed internally and their kidneys fail. A bite from this snake is not a nice way to die!

> **?** How is this snake more vicious than the other snakes you've read about?

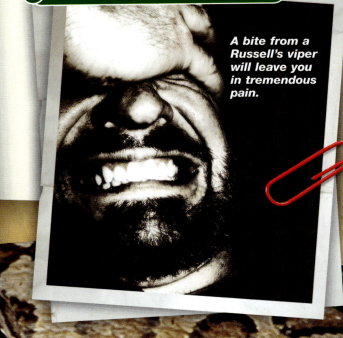

*A bite from a Russell's viper will leave you in tremendous pain.*

### The Expert Says...

" We have both the Russell's viper and the cobra in this area. The viper is much more dangerous — it is vicious. The cobra when confronted will rear its head and then run away; the viper will always make a stand and perhaps strike several times. "

— Professor May Myint Win, quoted in *The Myanmar Times*

# SNAKE SLAUGHTER

AN ARTICLE BY MARK O'SHEA, HERPETOLOGIST

After reading this book, you might be thinking that the only good snake is a dead snake, right?

Wrong! Snakes are nature's pest controllers. They prey on rats, mice, and other animals that can spread disease and famine in human populations. Every year, many more people die of malnutrition and diseases associated with vermin than from venomous snakebites.

In Southeast Asia, huge numbers of snakes are collected for their skins and their meat. Some are drowned in bags to avoid damaging their hides.

Others are slit open while alive so their beating hearts can be removed and eaten.

Snake restaurants have become popular tourist stops. Sadly, tourists do not realize the environmental damage and cruelty involved in their "once in a lifetime meal." If these restaurants sold tiger or rhino meat, there would be an uproar.

This would never happen in North America, though. Could it? You bet. In the United States, the rattlesnake roundup began as a way to protect livestock in cattle country. It is now a multimillion-dollar tourist attraction. There are rattlesnake-eating competitions and events to see who can stuff the most live rattlesnakes into a sack. Thousands of rattlesnakes are needed for these events. Sometimes they are even brought in from other places. This goes against the original reason for the round-up. Also, the removal of rattlesnakes (and the ways they are removed) can seriously damage the habitat for many species, not just rattlesnakes.

It is not a crime to be a snake. They play an important part in the natural ecology of our world. So if you see a snake, don't reach for the nearest rock to kill it. Stand back, marvel at its design, and then let it go on its way.

vermin: *small animals or insects that are pests to humans*

### Quick Fact
The Russell's viper has one of the loudest hisses of any snake. This is due to its large nostrils that act like a trumpet flare, projecting the sound.

### Take Note
The Russell's viper ranks #1 on our list for many reasons. It doesn't give a person a chance to back away before it attacks, and it has killed many people. When people replaced forests with fields to grow their crops, they destroyed the Russell's viper's natural habitat. The snake now hunts in these fields, and many workers are bitten.
- Does the fact that its original habitat was destroyed change the way you think about the Russell's viper and the other deadly snakes in this book? Explain.

## We Thought …

Here are the criteria we used in ranking the 10 deadliest snakes.

**The snake:**
- Has powerful venom
- Has an unusual or aggressive personality
- Is able to attack and eat large prey
- Lives close to humans
- Is able to blend into and hide in its environment
- Has unique methods of killing
- Has a mythology developed surrounding its deadliness

## What Do You Think?

1. Do you agree with our ranking? If you don't, try ranking the snakes yourself. Justify your ranking with data from your own research and reasoning. You may refer to our criteria, or you may want to draw up your own list of criteria.

2. Here are three other snakes that we considered but in the end did not include in our top 10 list: the king cobra, the anaconda, and the tropical rattlesnake.
   - Find out more about them. Do you think they should have made our list? Give reasons for your response.
   - Are there other snakes that you think should have made our list? Explain your choices.

# Index

## A
Africa, 27–29, 36
Aggressive, 23–25, 28, 31, 35–36, 46
Amputation, 25
Antibodies, 33
Antivenom, 9, 13–14, 16, 25, 28–29, 33
Asia, 40, 44–45
Australia, 7–8, 12–13, 16, 19–21, 23–25

## B
Bandicoot, 20
Bangkok, 41
Birds, 12, 16, 24, 28
Black mamba, 13, 26–29, 33
Bloodstream, 9, 17
Brown snake, 13, 22–25, 29
Buachan, Boonreung, 41
Burrows, 8, 28

## C
Camouflaged, 16, 36–37
Cannibalistic, 32
Centipedes, 41
Chaibuddee, Khum, 41
China, 44
Circulatory system, 25
Coastal taipan, 13, 18–21, 25
Cobras, 13, 25, 28, 30, 33, 38–41, 44, 47
Cole, Barbara, 29
Common krait, 13, 30–33, 37
Constriction, 12
Corwin, Jeff, 28

## D
Death adder, 13–17, 21
Della-Flora, Rudy, 25

## E
Earth, 7–8, 21
Eastern brown snake, 22–25, 29
Eastern diamondback rattlesnake, 33
Eipper, Scott, 12
Elephant, 41
Enzymes, 25
Extinction, 12

## F
Fangs, 4, 8, 11–12, 17, 20, 23–25, 28–29, 32, 36, 40, 43
Fish, 4, 12
Frogs, 12, 16, 24, 32, 36, 40

## G
Guinea pigs, 20

## H
Haast, Bill, 33, 36
Hamid, Shahimi Abdul, 41
Headaches, 21
Hemotoxins, 25
Hood, 13, 28, 39–40
Human settlement, 8–9, 19, 44
Hypodermic needle, 17

## I
India, 32, 36, 40
Indian cobra, 13, 38–41
Indonesia, 16, 44
Inland taipan, 6–9, 13, 17, 19–20, 23

## K
King cobra, 28, 41, 47
Kraits, 13, 25, 30–33, 37

## L
Lizards, 12, 24, 32, 36, 40

## M
Malaysia, 41
Mambas, 17, 25
Marsupials, 20
Middle East, 36
Mseswa, Sibusiso, 29

## N
Nepal, 40
Nervous system, 25
Neurotoxins, 25
New Guinea, 16, 20, 24
Nocturnal, 32, 37

## O
Outback, 6, 8

## P
Painkiller, 28
Pakistan, 32, 40, 44
Papua New Guinea, 24
Paralyzed, 33
Pets, 9
Predators, 25
Prey, 7–8, 11–12, 15–17, 21, 24–25, 28, 32, 36, 38, 40, 45–46
Proteins, 25, 37

## R
Rain forests, 40
Rattle, 4, 35
Reflexes, 4, 19, 43
Reptiles, 8, 16
Respiratory system, 8, 25
Russell's viper, 13, 42–45

## S
Saliva, 25
Saw-scaled viper, 13, 33–37, 41
Scales, 35–36, 40
Scorpions, 36, 41
Sharma, Suresh Captain, 32
Shine, Richard, 8
Siamese cobra, 33
Skin, 4, 32, 40, 45
Snake charmer, 39–41
Sri Lanka, 32, 36–37, 40
Stolze, Bruno, 21
Swamps, 12
Symptoms, 9, 21, 32–33

## T
Thailand, 41
Tiger snake, 10–13, 17
Tissue, 21, 33
Toxic, 8–9, 12, 16–19, 23, 25, 43–44

## U
United States, 37, 45

## V
Venom sacs, 19–21, 40
Viper, 13, 25, 33–37, 41, 44–45

## W
Wakefield, Ann, 21
Weigel, John, 16
Whitaker, Romulus, 40
Win, May Myint, 44
Wolf snake, 32
Worm, 3, 16